RAILWAYS IN DEVON AND CORNWALL
IN THE LATE 20TH CENTURY

RAILWAYS IN DEVON AND CORNWALL
IN THE LATE 20TH CENTURY

PETER J. GREEN

AN IMPRINT OF PEN & SWORD BOOKS LTD.
YORKSHIRE – PHILADELPHIA

First published in Great Britain in 2025 by
Pen and Sword Transport
An imprint of
Pen & Sword Books Ltd.
Yorkshire - Philadelphia

Copyright © Peter J. Green, 2025

ISBN 978 1 39903 429 6

The right of Peter J. Green to be identified as author of this work has been asserted by him in accordance with the Copyright, Designs and Patents Act 1988.

A CIP catalogue record for this book is available from the British Library.

All rights reserved. No part of this book may be reproduced, transmitted, downloaded, decompiled or reverse engineered in any form or by any means, electronic or mechanical including photocopying, recording or by any information storage and retrieval system, without permission from the Publisher in writing. NO AI TRAINING: Without in any way limiting the Author's and Publisher's exclusive rights under copyright, any use of this publication to "train" generative artificial intelligence (AI) technologies to generate text is expressly prohibited. The Author and Publisher reserve all rights to license uses of this work for generative AI training and development of machine learning language models.

Typeset by SJmagic DESIGN SERVICES, India.

The Publisher's authorised representative in the EU for product safety is Authorised Rep Compliance Ltd., Ground Floor, 71 Lower Baggot Street, Dublin D02 P593, Ireland.
www.arccompliance.com

For a complete list of Pen & Sword titles please contact

PEN & SWORD BOOKS LIMITED
George House, Beevor Street, Off Pontefract Road, Hoyle Mill, Barnsley,
South Yorkshire, England, S71 1HN.
E-mail: enquiries@pen-and-sword.co.uk
Website: www.pen-and-sword.co.uk

or

PEN AND SWORD BOOKS
1950 Lawrence Rd, Havertown, PA 19083, USA
E-mail: uspen-and-sword@casematepublishers.com
Website: www.penandswordbooks.com

CONTENTS

Acknowledgements 7

Introduction 8

Map of the Railways of Devon and Cornwall 10

Taunton to Cowley Bridge Junction 11

Cowley Bridge Junction to Barnstaple, Meeth and Meldon Quarry 22

Cowley Bridge Junction to Exeter St Davids 38

Exeter St Davids to Axminster 44

Exmouth Junction to Exmouth 63

Exeter to Newton Abbot 67

Newton Abbot to Heathfield 86

Newton Abbot to Aller Junction 90

Aller Junction to Paignton 96

Aller Junction to Plymouth and Keyham 103

The Gunnislake Branch 118

Saltash to Liskeard 124

Liskeard to Looe 131

Liskeard to Bodmin Parkway 137

Bodmin Parkway to Wenford Bridge 142

Lostwithiel to Carne Point 146

Lostwithiel to Par 149

Par to Newquay 157

St Austell to Burngullow including the freight line from
Burngullow Junction 165

Burngullow Junction to Truro 171

Truro to Falmouth 173

Truro to St Erth 176

St Erth to St Ives 184

St Erth to Penzance 187

Steam on the Main Line in 1985 191

Preserved Railways 194

Bibliography 203

Index 204

ACKNOWLEDGEMENTS

While the majority of photographs in this book are my own or from my personal collection, it has been my good fortune that a number of other railway photographers have allowed me to use their excellent photos of locations that I did not visit or of workings that I did not see. So here, I would like to express my gratitude to Max Birchenough, Paul Dorney, Don Gatehouse, David Rostance, Steve Turner, John Whitehouse, John Whiteley and Steve Widdowson who have all contributed photos to this book.

The railways of Cornwall are known for their viaducts. Because I was concerned about my lack of photos of them, before I decided to go ahead with this book I had a discussion with Steve Turner who allayed my fears and has provided some of his own, in addition to various other photos. These have certainly improved the balance of the book.

I have also received considerable assistance with my captions from David J. Hayes, with his knowledge of freight workings, as well as James Billingham, Paul Dorney, Don Gatehouse, David Rostance and Steve Turner.

As usual, Val Brown has checked the text and corrected the mistakes I have made.

My thanks go to you all.

Peter J. Green

INTRODUCTION

It was during a family holiday in Devon in 1959 that my passion for railways began. The sight and sound of the trains running along the coast at Dawlish and Teignmouth was too much for a young boy to resist and I soon began collecting numbers. At that time, almost all of the trains were steam-hauled but the occasional diesel would appear. While their new look was also appealing, it was some years later that my interest in modern traction really took off.

It was not long before I started photographing the railways, but I still regret not bothering with the Warship and Hymek diesel-hydraulics which regularly passed through my home town of Worcester. Some compensation for this omission was provided by a few visits to Devon in the mid-1970s to see the Western Class diesel-hydraulics running along the coast. They were being replaced by Class 50 diesel-electrics at the time. I can well remember what a pleasure it was to visit again those places that I had become familiar with all those years before.

In the 1970s and early 1980s, I spent more time in Devon, photographing the Torbay Steam Railway and the Dart Valley Railway, and an Easter camping trip to Goodrington became a regular event for several years. Of course, diesels were photographed as well during these visits, as time permitted.

From 1983, the 1986 West of England resignalling scheme provided a a good reason for a further series of visits to Devon, usually with groups of like-minded enthusiasts, to record the mechanical signal boxes, semaphore signalling and associated equipment before it all disappeared.

My first railway holiday in Cornwall was in the summer of 1984, when I spent ten days trying to photograph the entire Cornish railway system! A very enjoyable but impossible task, of course. Nevertheless, the Class 37s on the china clay operations, as well as all the 'Peaks' and Class 50s on the main line, ensured that I had a good time. Many more trips were made to Cornwall, some lasting a few days, while others were just day trips. Living not far from the M5 motorway in Worcester made access to the West Country fast and easy.

My photographs in this book were taken with a variety of cameras, including Pentax MX and medium format Mamiya 645 1000S Single Lens Reflexes (SLRs). Many of the earliest photos were taken with a Minolta SRT101 35 mm SLR using Ilford FP4 film.

I have attempted to give good coverage of the two counties in this book, from the mid-1970s until the turn of the century and, in order to achieve that, I have also included some high quality photographs from various other sources.

Peter J. Green

Worcester,
England,
2024

10 • RAILWAYS IN DEVON AND CORNWALL IN THE LATE 20TH CENTURY

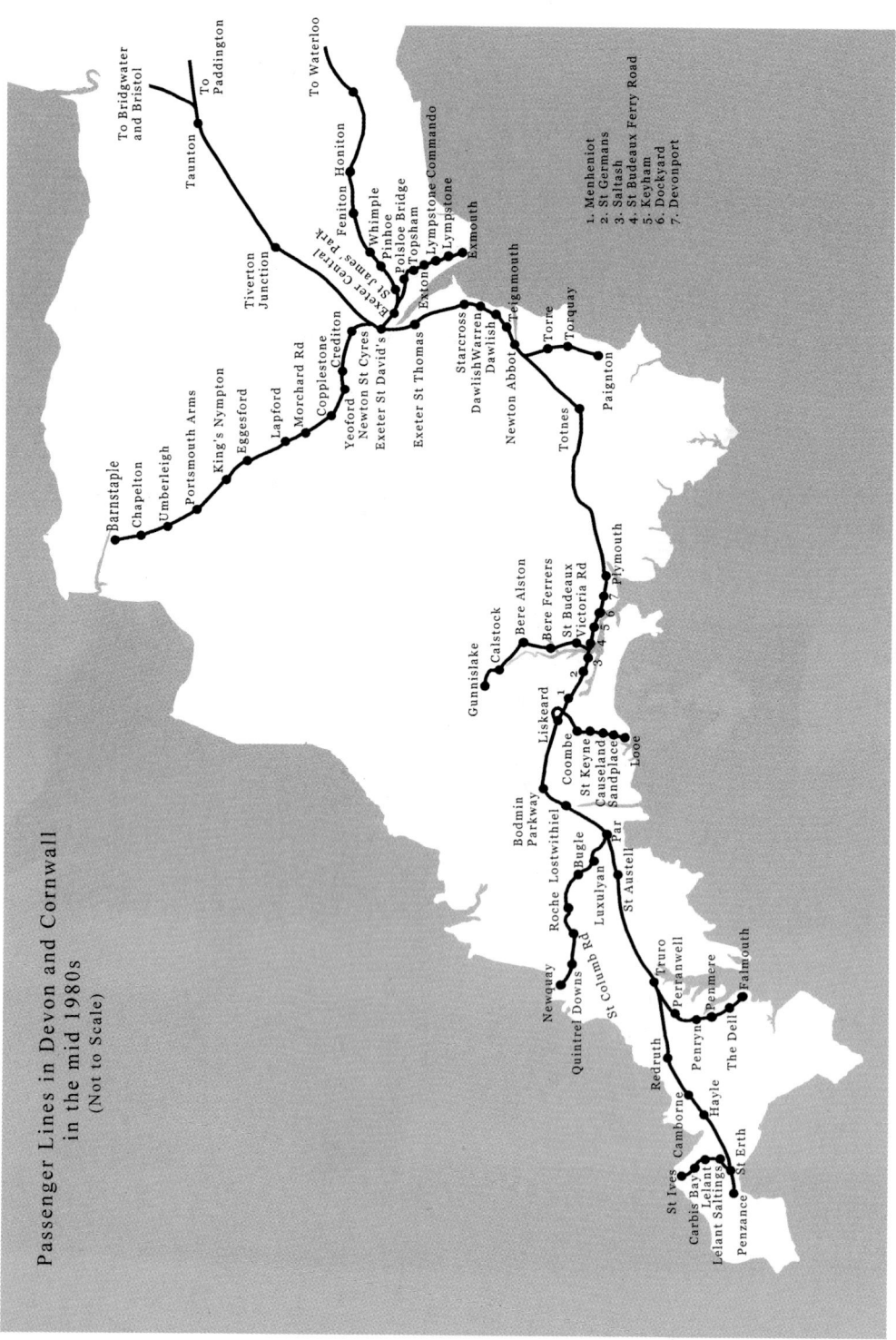

Map of passenger lines in Devon and Cornwall in the 1980s. For clarity, freight lines and heritage railways are not included.

TAUNTON TO COWLEY BRIDGE JUNCTION

While I had visited Devon and Cornwall on a number of occasions before, the 1986 West of England resignalling scheme, which saw the semaphore signals on the former Great Western Railway (GWR) line between Taunton and Exeter replaced, prompted a further series of visits to record as much as possible before it was too late. These visits often commenced at Taunton in Somerset, before I headed further west. Here, Class 117 three-car diesel multiple unit (DMU) set B436 passes under the 40 Steps signal gantry at the west end of Taunton station, as it heads for Wellington and on to Devon. The signals were removed from the gantry in April 1986. 18 August 1984.

Heading south-west through Somerset on the former GWR main line towards Devon, Class 50 50041 *Bulwark* passes Wellington station, closed in 1964, with the 1C23 09.07 London Paddington to Paignton, 'Torbay Express'. The GWR Type 7 signal box closed in 1986. 14 September 1985.

Opposite above: **The county boundary** between Somerset and Devon crosses Whiteball Tunnel. Having entered the tunnel in Somerset, Class 45 'Peak' 45115 exits the tunnel in Devon with the 1V67 07.59 Nottingham to Paignton. Whiteball Siding signal box was rebuilt in 1955, using the original 1876 Saxby & Farmer Type 4 base. It was closed in 1986. 14 September 1985.

Opposite below: **Class 50 50045** *Achilles* approaches Tiverton Junction station with a northbound empty stock working to Old Oak Common. 14 July 1985.

TAUNTON TO COWLEY BRIDGE JUNCTION • 13

Class 45 'Peak' 45077 passes Tiverton Junction station with the 1M65 16.08 Paignton to Liverpool Lime Street. The station, located at Willand and closed in May 1986, was once the junction station for the line to Tiverton and the Culm Valley line. The signal box is a standard GWR design. 18 August 1984.

Opposite above: **Class 50 50027** *Lion* heads the 1V84 13.06 Birmingham New Street to Paignton through Tiverton Junction station. 6 August 1983.

Opposite below: **Class 45 'Peak'** 45148 heads through Tiverton Junction station with an unidentified southbound parcels train. 18 August 1984.

TAUNTON TO COWLEY BRIDGE JUNCTION • **15**

Above: **Class 37 diesel-electrics** 37674 and 37412 head the 6V70 08.28 SO Bescot to St. Blazey china clay empties towards Tiverton Parkway station. The station was opened in May 1986, on the site of the former Sampford Peverell Halt, when Tiverton Junction station was closed. The train is made up of 'Polybulk' hoppers instead of the usual PBA 'Tigers' because Tiger Rail had recently gone out of business. This train was a forwarding connection of 6G56, the 17.15 FO Cliffe Vale to Bescot. 25 April 1992.

Opposite above: **Class 59 59004** *Yeoman Challenger* heads north, next to the M5 motorway near Cullompton, with Pathfinder Tours' returning 'Plym Exe-Cursioner' railtour from Manchester Piccadilly to Plymouth. Based on the succesful North American SD40-2 type of which nearly 4,000 were produced, the locomotive was built by the Electro-Motive Division of General Motors for Foster Yeoman, entering service in 1986. 1 May 1994.

Opposite below: **Class 50 50031** *Hood* passes Cullompton with Pathfinder Tours' 'The Taw Tor Retourer' from Manchester Piccadilly to Barnstaple, Exmouth and Heathfield. This railtour was a rerun of 'The Taw Tor Tourer' of 5 May 1990, which did not reach Barnstaple. Opened in 1844, Cullompton station closed to passengers in October 1964, but goods traffic continued until the following year. 16 September 1990.

TAUNTON TO COWLEY BRIDGE JUNCTION • 17

Above: **InterCity 125 unit** set 253 030, forming an unidentified eastbound working, passes the closed station of Hele and Bradninch. 1 September 1985.

Opposite above: **Class 50 50008** *Thunderer* heads west past Hele and Bradninch with the 1C20 09.32 Cardiff Central to Plymouth. Hele and Bradninch station was opened as Hele in 1844. Passenger services were withdrawn in October 1964 with freight continuing until May 1965. The Bristol and Exeter Railway signal box closed in December 1985, when control passed to the new panel signal box at Exeter. 8 September 1985.

Opposite below: **Class 45 'Peak'** 45146 passes Stoke Canon with the 1Z44 09.38 Derby to Plymouth 'FootEx'. The special train ran in connection with a football match between Plymouth Argyle and Derby County, where the final score was Derby County 1-0 Plymouth Argyle. 16 March 1985.

TAUNTON TO COWLEY BRIDGE JUNCTION • 19

Class 50 50016 *Barham* passes Stoke Canon Crossing signal box, located at Green Lane, with the 08.15 additional working from Penzance to London Paddington. The Saxby and Farmer box, built in 1876 for the Bristol and Exeter Railway, was closed in December 1985. It is now a listed building. A station opened at Stoke Canon in 1860 and was closed in 1960. 24 August 1984.

Opposite: **With the Cowley** Bridge Inn on the right, Class 47/4 47575 *City of Hereford* passes Cowley Bridge Junction with the 1Z90 09.30 Bristol Temple Meads to Exeter St Davids relief working. Located north of Exeter St Davids, it is the junction of the former Bristol and Exeter Railway and the Exeter and Crediton Railway. The Exeter and Crediton Railway later became part of the London and South Western Railway (LSWR). 1 May 1994.

COWLEY BRIDGE JUNCTION TO BARNSTAPLE, MEETH AND MELDON QUARRY

Opposite: **After crossing the** River Exe, token duties are carried out at the end of the single line as Class 118 three-car DMU set P461, forming the 10.38 Barnstaple to Exeter St Davids service, arrives at Cowley Bridge Junction signal box. Opened in 1894, replacing an earlier box, it was closed in 1985. From time to time, flooding of the River Exe in this area caused disruption to rail services. 16 March 1985.

Below: **Class 33/1 'Cromptons'** 33114 and 33102 approach Newton St Cyres station, between Crediton and Exeter, with a loaded stone train from Meldon Quarry. 30 July 1990.

24 • RAILWAYS IN DEVON AND CORNWALL IN THE LATE 20TH CENTURY

Opposite above: **Class 33/0 'Crompton'** 33008 *Eastleigh* passes Newton St Cyres station with stone empties bound for Meldon Quarry. The station was opened by the Exeter and Crediton Railway in 1851. The locomotive has been repainted into early green livery with a yellow warning panel. 30 August 1989.

Opposite below: **Class 118 three-car** DMU set P469, forming a Barnstaple to Exmouth service, pauses at Crediton. The station, opened in 1851, is the junction of the lines to Barnstaple and Meldon Quarry, although the two lines run in parallel until the former Coleford Junction at Penstone. 17 September 1985.

The crew of Class 33/0 'Crompton' 33065 prepare to exchange tokens at Crediton signal box, as they arrive with a loaded stone train from Meldon Quarry. The lever frame was removed from the box and a control panel fitted in December 1984. 30 August 1989.

Above: **Class 33/0 'Crompton'** 33065 heads an empty stone train to Meldon Quarry through Yeoford station. The line on the left leads to Barnstaple. The station was opened by the North Devon Railway in 1857. 30 August 1989.

Opposite above: **In early Network** SouthEast livery, Class 50 50037 *Illustrious* runs through the countryside near Yeoford, with a loaded stone train from Meldon Quarry. The quarry was opened in 1874 to supply ballast and other stone products to meet local railway needs. It was later developed to provide most of the ballast requirements of the LSWR. It was sold to ECC Quarries Ltd in 1994. 1 August 1989.

Opposite below: **Class 33/0 'Crompton'** 33038 heads away from Okehampton with stone from Meldon Quarry. Okehampton, once a busy junction station with lines to Padstow, Bude and Plymouth, was opened by the LSWR in 1871 and closed in 1972. In 2021, the station again became part of the national railway network. 19 September 1985.

COWLEY BRIDGE JUNCTION TO BARNSTAPLE, MEETH AND MELDON QUARRY • **27**

***Opposite above*: Class 33/0 'Crompton'** 33022 heads stone empties to Meldon Quarry through Okehampton station. The signal box was opened by the Southern Railway in 1935, replacing an earlier LSWR box. Although it was taken out of use in 1972, the box still remains today. 18 September 1985.

***Opposite below*: Class 33/1 'Cromptons'** 33102 and 33114 head the 7C53 09.15 Meldon Quarry to Exeter Riverside Yard loaded ballast train next to the A30 Okehampton Bypass, between the quarry and Okehampton station. 31 July 1990.

F & W Railtours' 1Z38 'The Devonshire Dart' railtour from Bristol Temple Meads visited various locations in Devon in July 1984. Here, after arriving at Meldon Quarry, the Class 20/0 diesel-electrics 20169 and 20184 are pictured running round their train before heading to Birmingham New Street. From there, 37176 and 37206 took the train back to Bristol Temple Meads. 8 July 1984. (*Steve Turner Photo*)

Continuing our journey along the line to Barnstaple from Crediton, Class 118 DMU set P467, forming a Barnstaple to Exeter Central service, arrives at Copplestone. The station was opened by the North Devon Railway in 1854. 17 September 1985.

Opposite above: **Class 108/101 hybrid** DMU set 870, forming the 13.01 Barnstaple to Exeter Central service, arrives at Lapford. The station was opened in 1855. 3 August 1990.

Opposite below: **Class 118 DMU** set P467, forming an Exmouth to Barnstaple service, arrives at Eggesford station. Opened in 1854, the station is around 22 miles from Exeter Central. The signal box was opened in 1969, replacing an earlier box, and controls the only crossing loop between Crediton and Barnstaple. 17 September 1985.

COWLEY BRIDGE JUNCTION TO BARNSTAPLE, MEETH AND MELDON QUARRY • 31

Class 118 DMU set P467, forming an Exmouth to Barnstaple service, departs from King's Nympton. The station was opened by the North Devon Railway as South Molton Road in 1854. It was renamed in 1951. 17 September 1985.

Opposite above: **Class 108/101 hybrid** DMU set 870, forming the 08.40 Exeter Central to Barnstaple service, arrives at Umberleigh. The station was opened by the North Devon Railway in 1854. 2 August 1990.

Opposite below: **Class 31/1 31232** passes Chapelton with the 6B26 11.10 Barnstaple to Exeter Riverside freight. The train is made up of empty cement wagons. Chapelton station was opened in 1854. 17 September 1985.

COWLEY BRIDGE JUNCTION TO BARNSTAPLE, MEETH AND MELDON QUARRY • 33

34 • RAILWAYS IN DEVON AND CORNWALL IN THE LATE 20TH CENTURY

Opposite above: **Class 118 DMU** set P480 stands at Barnstaple after arriving from Exeter Central. Approximately 39 miles from Exeter Central, the former LSWR station was opened in 1854. From 1874 until 1970, it was known as Barnstaple Junction. 17 September 1985.

Opposite below: **Class 118 DMU** set P480, forming a service to Exeter Central, has the road at Barnstaple station as it waits for its departure time. Barnstaple also had a GWR station, Victoria Road, and lines once ran from Barnstaple to Bideford, Taunton, and Ilfracombe, as well as to Exeter. The narrow gauge Lynton and Barnstaple Railway had its own station at Barnstaple Town. The line was closed by the Southern Railway in 1935. 17 September 1985.

Below: **Class 31/1 31174** with 15 coaches and 31158 on the rear stands at Torrington with British Rail's 'The Last Train to Torrington' railtour from Bristol Temple Meads. The station, opened in 1872, was closed in 1965. 6 November 1982. (*Steve Turner Photo*)

Eleven years before the previous photograph, North British Type 2 diesel-hydraulic 6334 arrives at Torrington with the 6C73 08.50 Barnstaple to Torrington and Meeth china clay empties. This type of locomotive was British Rail's Class 22 under the TOPS numbering system. 27 August 1971. (*John Medley Photo, Railphotoprints.co.uk*)

Swindon Cross-Country Class 120 DMU set B559 stands at the end of the line at Meeth, near the site of the former Meeth halt. The train is 'The Devon Rambler' railtour from Bristol Temple Meads, organised by the Bristol Branch of the RCTS. The line was closed to passenger traffic in 1965, but stayed open for freight from the Meeth clay workings, through Torrington to Barnstaple, until 1982. The line previously continued south to Halwill Junction and on to Bude and North Cornwall. The oil tank was used to hold fuel for lorries. 20 April 1974. (*Max Birchenough Photo*)

COWLEY BRIDGE JUNCTION TO EXETER ST DAVIDS

Class 45 'Peak' 45129 approaches Cowley Bridge Junction with the 1C82 13.54 Penzance to Bristol Temple Meads. On the right, infrastructure work is in progress for the West of England resignalling scheme. 16 March 1985.

Above: **InterCity 125 unit** set 253 004, forming a London Paddington to Penzance service, passes the fine bracket signal at the east end of the station, as it approaches Exeter St Davids. 6 August 1983.

Below: **An InterCity 125** unit, forming a London Paddington to Paignton service, passes the old goods shed as it arrives at Exeter St Davids. 6 August 1983.

Above: **With a PBA** 'Tiger' at the front of its short train, Class 45 45059 passes Exeter Middle signal box, at Red Cow level crossing, with a Riverside Yard to Heathfield china clay working. Exeter Middle signal box, located at the north end of Exeter St Davids station, was a GWR Type 31 design. Opened in 1914, it was closed in 1985. While Red Cow crossing was controlled by the signal box, in daylight hours an attendant was employed to assist pedestrians across the railway when the barriers were closed and it was safe to cross. The attendant is seen here talking to off duty railwaymen. 6 August 1984. (*Paul Dorney Photo*)

Opposite above: **Exeter Traction Maintenance** Depot (TMD) is located next to St Davids station. Present on the depot in this photograph are 50050 *Fearless*, 47804, 50045 *Achilles*, and 50009 *Conqueror*. An engine shed was built at Exeter by the Bristol and Exeter Railway in 1844, eventually closing in 1963 when the area was used as a fuelling and stabling point. In 1976, it became a depot once more and a new maintenance facility was built in 1980. 1 August 1990.

Opposite below: **Class 47/0 47285** arrives at Exeter St Davids with a train of milk tanks, bound for Lostwithiel for storage. The tanks did not see any further use and eventually were scrapped. 24 September 1984. (*Paul Dorney Photo*)

COWLEY BRIDGE JUNCTION TO EXETER ST DAVIDS • 41

Class 33/0 'Crompton' 33025 waits for the road at the north end of Exeter St Davids station, as Class 45 'Peak' 45133 departs with the 1M86 09.50 Paignton to Manchester Piccadilly. 6 August 1983.

Opposite above: Class 47/4 47589 departs from Exeter St Davids station with the 09.22 Newcastle to Penzance. Class 118 DMU set P462 stands alongside. Designed by Isambard Kingdom Brunel, Exeter St Davids station is just under 194 miles from London Paddington. It was opened in May 1844 by the Bristol and Exeter Railway. 16 March 1985.

Opposite below: Class 47/0 47248 crosses the River Exe and passes Exeter West signal box as it approaches Exeter St Davids station with the 1A69 12.10 Paignton to London Paddington. The lines on the left lead to Exeter Central. The box, originally built by the GWR in 1913, was closed in 1985. It is now preserved at the Crewe Heritage Centre, where demonstrations of the operation of a large mechanical signal box are given. 6 August 1983.

COWLEY BRIDGE JUNCTION TO EXETER ST DAVIDS • 43

EXETER ST DAVIDS TO AXMINSTER

Above: **Class 118 DMU** set P462, forming a local service from Exmouth to Exeter St Davids, runs down the gradient from Exeter Central as it approaches its destination. Exeter West signal box is on the right. 6 August 1983.

Opposite above: **Class 33/0 'Crompton'** 33018 crosses Bonhay Road and approaches St Davids Tunnel as it climbs the 1 in 37 gradient, from the former GWR Exeter St Davids station to the former LSWR Exeter Central station, with the 10.50 Penzance to Brighton. Exeter West signal box is in the background. 16 March 1985.

Opposite below: **Class 33/0 'Crompton'** 33025 *Sultan* departs from Exeter Central with an Exeter St Davids to London Waterloo service. Exeter Central signal box was built in 1927 to a standard Southern Railway design, but with a hipped roof, replacing two earlier boxes. After closure in 1985, the modern plate was removed from the end of the signal box, revealing the earlier 'Exeter Central A Box' plate, as can be seen in the next photograph. 6 August 1983.

EXETER ST DAVIDS TO AXMINSTER • 45

In revised Network SouthEast livery, Class 50 50028 *Tiger* departs from Exeter Central and passes the closed Exeter Central signal box with the 17.37 Exeter St Davids to London Waterloo. 30 July 1990.

Opposite above: Class 50 50046 *Ajax* passes under the Howell Road bridge as it heads away from Exeter Central with the 2O83 11.50 Exeter St Davids to London Waterloo. 29 June 1991.

Opposite below: Class 08 0-6-0 diesel-electric shunter 08576 approaches Exeter Central with a rake of empty 'Presflo' cement wagons from the nearby Blue Circle Cement terminal. The wagons are bound for Exeter Riverside Yard. 19 September 1985.

EXETER ST DAVIDS TO AXMINSTER • 47

Above: Class 50 50030 *Repulse* passes St James Park station, located ½ mile east of Exeter Central, with the 1O37 12.25 Exeter St Davids to London Waterloo. Opened in January 1906 and originally named Lion's Holt Halt, the name was changed to St James Park in 1946, the name of the nearby Exeter City F.C. ground. 29 June 1991.

Opposite above: Class 50 D400 50050 *Fearless* painted in its original BR blue livery and running without nameplates heads away from Blackboy Tunnel, near St James Park station, with the 1V15 15.15 London Waterloo to Exeter St Davids. The tunnel is 263 yards long. 29 June 1991.

Opposite below: Class 47/7 47709 exits the eastern portal of Blackboy Tunnel and heads towards Exmouth Junction with the 1O86 09.25 Plymouth to London Waterloo. 29 June 1991.

EXETER ST DAVIDS TO AXMINSTER • 49

Above: **Class 50 50007** *Sir Edward Elgar* passes Exmouth Junction coal depot as it heads away from the junction with the 1V10 11.14 Southampton to Plymouth. The locomotive, previously named *Hercules*, was renamed and painted in Brunswick Green in April 1984, ready for the 150th anniversary of the GWR the following year. 29 June 1991.

Opposite above: **With Exmouth Junction** in the background, a Class 118 DMU, forming an Exmouth to Exeter St Davids service, approaches Blackboy Tunnel. The Exmouth line can be seen curving away to the right in front of Exmouth Junction signal box. The box opened in November 1959, replacing an earlier one. The lever frame was replaced by a panel in 1988. 19 September 1985.

Opposite below: **Class 50 50027** *Lion* heads away from the Pinhoe station stop with the 2V05 06.05 Salisbury to Exeter St Davids. The station, on the eastern edge of Exeter, was opened by the LSWR in 1871. 29 June 1991.

EXETER ST DAVIDS TO AXMINSTER • 51

Class 50 50026 *Indomitable* pauses at Pinhoe with the 16.18 Exeter St Davids to London Waterloo service. 19 September 1985.

Opposite above: Class 33/0 'Crompton' 33008 *Eastleigh* approaches Pinhoe with the 7V84 13.05 Salisbury to Exeter Riverside stone empties. The train will later work forward as the 7B28 to Meldon Quarry. The LSWR Type 1 signal box, opened in 1875, was closed in February 1988, when it was purchased privately and moved to Bere Ferrers. 18 September 1985.

Opposite below: Class 50 50009 *Conqueror* passes the former Broad Clyst station with the 15.15 London Waterloo to Exeter St Davids. The station, which served the village of Broadclyst, was opened in 1860 by the LSWR. It was closed in 1966. 29 August 1989.

EXETER ST DAVIDS TO AXMINSTER • 53

Class 50 50027 *Lion* passes Whimple with a London Waterloo to Exeter St Davids service. The station, designed by Sir William Tite, was opened by the LSWR in July 1860, when it extended its line from Yeovil Junction to Exeter. 10 September 1988.

Opposite above: **Class 50 50002** *Superb* passes Whimple with an Exeter St Davids to London Waterloo service. Much of the goods traffic from Whimple originated from a cider factory opened by Henry Whiteway in 1892. The LSWR goods shed was demolished in 1991. 10 September 1988.

Opposite below: **Class 50 50044** *Exeter* rounds the curve near Talaton, between Whimple and Feniton, with a London Waterloo to Exeter St Davids service. Withdrawn from service in 1991, the locomotive was purchased by the Fifty Fund and is now preserved at the Severn Valley Railway (SVR), one of the eighteen members of the class that were saved for preservation. 10 September 1988.

EXETER ST DAVIDS TO AXMINSTER • 55

Class 50 50003 *Temeraire* heads away from Feniton, opened by the LSWR in 1860, with an Exeter St Davids to London Waterloo service. 10 September 1988.

Opposite above: **Class 50 50050** *Fearless* starts the 1O51 12.28 Exeter St Davids to London Waterloo away from the Honiton station stop. The station was opened in 1860. 29 August 1989.

Opposite below: **Class 50 50007** *Sir Edward Elgar* runs through attractive countryside near Wilmington, east of Honiton, with the 1V15 15.15 London Waterloo to Exeter St Davids. The locomotive is now preserved at the SVR. 13 April 1991.

EXETER ST DAVIDS TO AXMINSTER • 57

Above: **Class 33/1 'Crompton'** 33114 is pictured near Umborne, west of Seaton Junction, with the 07.45 Basingstoke to Exeter St Davids. 20 April 1991.

Opposite above: **Class 47/7 47709** rounds the curve near Seaton Junction with the 1O35 10.20 Exeter St Davids to London Waterloo. 13 July 1991.

Opposite below: **Class 33/1 'Crompton'** 33114 passes the closed Seaton Junction station with the 1O37 12.25 Exeter St Davids to London Waterloo. Opened in 1860 as Colyton for Seaton, Seaton Junction is between Honiton and Axminster. Closed in 1966, the section of the former branch line from Colyton to Seaton has been reopened as the narrow gauge Seaton Tramway. The Southern Railway's extensive use of concrete is evident in this photograph. 20 April 1991.

EXETER ST DAVIDS TO AXMINSTER • 59

Class 50 50002 *Superb* heads the 1V10 11.14 Southampton to Plymouth round a curve near Whitford. The locomotive was later preserved by the Devon Diesel Society. 20 April 1991.

Class 50 50014 *Warspite* arrives at Axminster with the 1O24 17.33 Exeter St Davids to London Waterloo. The station, the last in Devon on the former Southern Railway route to London Waterloo, was opened in 1860 by the LSWR. 2 September 1986. (*John Whitehouse Photo*)

Class 50 50005 *Collingwood* is pictured near Weycroft as it heads away from Axminster and towards the county boundary between Devon and Dorset, with the 16.22 Exeter St Davids to London Waterloo. 31 August 1989.

EXMOUTH JUNCTION TO EXMOUTH

The line to Exmouth was opened by the LSWR in 1861 and became part of the Southern Railway in 1923. Here, Class 118 DMU set P469, forming an Exeter St Davids to Exmouth service, approaches Polsoe Bridge station. Opened in 1907, the station serves Exeter's eastern suburbs. Exmouth Junction locomotive depot was nearby. 19 September 1985.

64 • RAILWAYS IN DEVON AND CORNWALL IN THE LATE 20TH CENTURY

Opposite above: **Class 118 DMU** set P471, forming an Exeter St Davids to Exmouth service, arrives at Topsham station. The station has the only crossing loop on the single line between Exmouth Junction and Exmouth. The signal box, opened circa 1870, is a LSWR modified Type 1 design. Closed in 1988, it is now Grade II listed, as are the station buildings. 19 September 1985.

Opposite below: **A single passenger** waits on the platform as Class 118 DMU set P471, forming an Exeter St Davids to Exmouth service, arrives at Topsham. Opened in 1861, the station buildings were designed by Sir William Tite. A short branch line once ran from here to a wharf on the River Exe. 19 September 1985.

Below: **Skipper 142 018,** forming the 18.45 Exmouth to Exeter St Davids service, crosses the low viaduct at Lympstone as it approaches the station. 5 September 1986. (*John Whitehouse Photo*)

Class 118 DMU set P461 waits at Exmouth for its departure time to Exeter St Davids. The railway to Exmouth was opened in 1861, when the original station consisted of a single platform with two faces. In 1924, it was rebuilt with four platforms. A line once ran from Exmouth to Sidmouth Junction on the former LSWR line from London Waterloo to Exeter. 19 September 1985.

EXETER TO NEWTON ABBOT

The scenic former GWR line from Exeter to Newton Abbot runs alongside the River Exe estuary and the Devon coast as far as Teignmouth. Here, in InterCity livery and with a train of InterCity stock, Class 47/8 47804 heads towards Exminster with the 12.35 London Paddington to Penzance. 31 July 1990.

Above: **Class 47/0 47089** heads for Exeter, past the semaphore signals to the north of Exminster, with the 1E32 16.43 Paignton to Leeds as Class 50 50040 *Leviathan* approaches with the 1C52 14.27 London Paddington to Penzance. 14 September 1985.

Opposite above: **With power car** 43184 leading, an InterCity 125 unit passes the site of Exminster station, as it heads south towards Starcross. The station was closed to passengers in 1964 and to goods three years later. The signal box, originally built in 1924, was extended a number of times, the last time being in 1941 when it was fitted with an 80-lever frame. It was closed in November 1986 but remained in place until 2006. 6 October 1984.

Opposite below: **Viewed from the** Station Road bridge, Class 31/1 31297 passes Exminster as it heads the afternoon Plymouth to Leeds parcels towards Exeter. The former station building, just out of the picture on the right, is now a private residence. 6 October 1984.

EXETER TO NEWTON ABBOT • 69

Above: **Class 47/8 47839** runs alongside the River Exe estuary as it approaches Starcross with a service to Paignton. 29 June 1991.

Opposite above: **Class 50 diesel-electrics** D400 (50050 *Fearless,* running without nameplates) and 50049 *Defiance* head the 2C08 07.12 Newton Abbot to Exeter St Davids away from Starcross station. The former pumping station for Brunel's Atmospheric Railway between Exeter and Newton Abbot can be seen in the background. 29 June 1991.

Opposite below: **Viewed from the** top of the former pumping station for Brunel's Atmospheric Railway, the 1C36 12.35 London Paddington to Penzance passes Starcross station behind Class 47/8 47848 in InterCity livery. The River Exe estuary is on the right. 28 July 1990.

EXETER TO NEWTON ABBOT • 71

Above: **Class 50 50009** *Conqueror* passes Cockwood Harbour, just south of Starcross, with the 1A91 17.45 Paignton to London Paddington. 15 July 1989.

Opposite above: **Class 52 'Western'** diesel-hydraulic 1071 *Western Renown* takes the middle road, as it heads the 1B55 12.30 London Paddington to Paignton, through Dawlish Warren station. The station was opened by the GWR in September 1912, replacing a halt located a short distance away. *Western Renown* was one of the few Class 52s which had a grille fitted to the front of the locomotive to improve cab ventilation. 16 April 1974.

Opposite below: **Class 45 'Peak'** 45137 *The Bedfordshire & Hertfordshire Regiment* heads the 1V82 10.23 Manchester Piccadilly to Penzance through the Down middle road at Dawlish Warren. The GWR signal box closed in November 1986. 29 August 1981.

EXETER TO NEWTON ABBOT • **73**

Above: Viewed from Langstone Rock, Class 52 'Western' diesel-hydraulic 1055 *Western Advocate* rounds the curve near Dawlish Warren as it heads towards Dawlish with an unidentified freight working. Fitted with two Maybach MD655 engines producing a total of 2,700 bhp, seventy-four of these Type 4 C-C locomotives were built between 1961 and 1964 at Swindon and Crewe Works for the Western Region. The class was withdrawn from service between 1973 and 1977, with seven locomotives surviving into preservation. 31 March 1975.

Opposite above: With Dawlish in the background, Class 37/5 diesel-electrics 37672 *Freight Transport Association* and 37670 assist an InterCity 125 unit past Langstone Rock. The working is the 07.35 Penzance to London Paddington. The locomotives were removed from the train at Exeter St Davids. 26 August 1989.

Opposite below: Class 52 'Western' diesel-hydraulic 1059 *Western Empire* heads east along the sea wall at Dawlish. The 7S38 headcode indicates that the working is the 11.05 St Blazey to Glasgow Sighthill. The train includes 16-ton mineral wagons, china clay wagons and two clayhoods. 31 March 1975.

EXETER TO NEWTON ABBOT • 75

An **InterCity 125** unit, forming a London Paddington to Penzance service, heads along the sea wall from Dawlish Warren as it approaches Dawlish station. Langstone Rock is in the background. 15 September 1985.

Opposite above: **Class 50 50026,** as yet unnamed, heads the 1M22 11.22 Plymouth to Manchester Piccadilly through Dawlish station. The locomotive was named *Indomitable* on 29 March 1978. Withdrawn in 1990, it was rescued for preservation from Booth's scrapyard at Rotherham in 1993. 1 April 1975.

Opposite below: **Power car 43179** leads InterCity 125 unit set 253 049, forming a Paignton to Manchester Piccadilly service, into Dawlish station. The signal box, opened in 1920, was used on an as required basis from 1970, normally on Saturdays in the summer, until it was taken out of use in September 1986. The box, a listed building, was demolished in 2013 because of its poor condition. 6 October 1984.

EXETER TO NEWTON ABBOT • 77

Class 52 'Western' diesel-hydraulic 1070 *Western Gauntlet* starts the 1B33 14.30 London Paddington to Penzance away from the Dawlish station stop. The station was opened on Brunel's broad gauge railway by the South Devon Railway in 1846. The South Devon Railway became part of the GWR in 1876, and in 1892 the line was converted to standard gauge. 7 September 1975.

Opposite above: **Class 47/0 47147** makes a smoky departure from Dawlish with the 1V67 06.43 Leeds City to Paignton. Originally numbered D1740, the locomotive was cut up at Vic Berry's scrapyard in 1993. 29 March 1975.

Opposite below: **With only a** few people strolling along the sea wall, Class 47/4 47547 leaves Kennaway Tunnel as it arrives at Dawlish with the 1A48 11.05 Paignton to London Paddington. The tunnel, beneath Lea Mount, is 265 yards long and is the first of five tunnels between Dawlish and Teignmouth. 6 October 1984.

EXETER TO NEWTON ABBOT • **79**

Above: **With Dawlish in** the background, Class 50 50038 *Formidable* exits Clerk's Tunnel, 58yd long, as it heads for Teignmouth with the 1C37 11.45 London Paddington to Penzance. The beach above the locomotive, protected by a breakwater, is at Shell Cove, with Horse Rocks on the right. This location has often been described as Horse Cove. 15 September 1985.

Opposite above: **Class 52 'Western'** diesel-hydraulic 1058 *Western Nobleman* exits Parson's Tunnel and is about to cross Smugglers Lane as it heads for Teignmouth with the 1B35 10.30 London Paddington to Paignton. The tunnel is 513yd long and is the last of the five tunnels between Dawlish and Teignmouth. 31 March 1975.

Opposite below: **Class 45 'Peak'** 45004 heads along the sea wall, away from Teignmouth and towards Parson's Tunnel, with the 6C39 09.34 St Blazey to Severn Tunnel Junction Speedlink service. The train is made up of a PBA china clay 'Tiger', vans probably containing bagged clay, and a clay slurry tanker. There are also PCA cement tanks at the rear. 20 September 1985.

EXETER TO NEWTON ABBOT • 81

Above: **With car transporters** at the rear of the train, Class 52 'Western' diesel-hydraulic 1041 *Western Prince* approaches Teignmouth with the 1V34 Kensington Olympia to St Austell Motorail. 31 March 1975.

Opposite above: **Passing under Eastcliff** Walk, Class 52 'Western' diesel-hydraulic 1052 *Western Viceroy* rounds the curve on to the sea wall from Teignmouth station with the 1A05 11.55 Paignton to London Paddington. 31 March 1975.

Opposite below: **Class 47/4 47497** arrives at Teignmouth with the 1E91 08.55 Penzance to Newcastle. The GWR Teignmouth signal box, on the left, was closed in November 1986 and demolished the following February. 18 September 1985.

EXETER TO NEWTON ABBOT • **83**

Above: **Class 47/0 47106** heads the St Austell to London Paddington Motorail service through Teignmouth station. At this time, the cars were carried on a separate working, with passengers travelling on an InterCity 125 unit to London. 6 August 1983.

Below: **Viewed from Shaldon** Bridge, Teignmouth, Class 50 50028 *Tiger* heads the 1C20 09.32 Cardiff Central to Plymouth alongside the River Teign estuary towards Newton Abbot. 15 September 1985.

Above: **Class 66 66049** approaches Shaldon Bridge with Saturday's Burngullow to Irvine china clay slurry tanks. At this date, the train was booked to run to Warrington Arpley, from where it went forward as the 6S55 17:00 SuO to Irvine. 23 September 2000.

Below: **With Newton Abbot** East signal box visible above the train, an InterCity 125 unit passes under the signal gantry at the east end of Newton Abbot station. The buildings on the left are the former maltings of Edwin Tucker and Sons Ltd. 6 October 1984.

NEWTON ABBOT TO HEATHFIELD

Heathfield station, originally named Chudleigh Road, was located on the Moretonhampstead and South Devon Railway, just under 4 miles from Newton Abbot. Regular passenger traffic ended in 1959.

Here, after arriving at Newton Abbot with a china clay train from Heathfield, Class 31/4 31404 has run round its train and is waiting to depart to Exeter Riverside yard. 6 August 1985. (*Paul Dorney Photo*)

Newton Abbot station was opened by the South Devon Railway Company on 30 December 1846. To celebrate its 150th anniversary, a number of special trains ran on the Heathfield branch at Rail 150 Newton Abbot. Here, Class 37/4 37416 trails at the rear of one of the Heathfield shuttles as the train approaches Newton Abbot. Class 37/5 37668 is leading. 31 December 1996.

Above: **Pathfinder Tours ran** 'The Taw Retourer' from Manchester Piccadilly to Barnstaple, Exmouth and Heathfield in September 1990. Between Bristol Temple Meads and Exeter St Davids, 50031 *Hood* was the motive power, while 50032 *Courageous* returned the train to Bristol. The two 50s ran top and tail on the Devon branches. Here, *Hood* is pictured on the Heathfield branch approaching Newton Abbot with the returning special. *Courageous* is out of sight on the rear of the train. 16 September 1990.

Opposite above: **Class 33/0 'Crompton'** 33043 is about to cross Exeter Road at Teignbridge Crossing with a china clay train returning from Heathfield. The former crossing keeper's cottage is on the left. 14 February 1986. (*Paul Dorney Photo*)

Opposite below: **From July 1970,** Heathfield was the terminus of the branch and saw trains running to an oil terminal located there. Here, Class 37/0 37141 stands in the former Heathfield station with the 6Z20 12.05 Heathfield Gulf Oil to Swansea Burrows Sidings. This was the final tank train from Heathfield. 17 January 1996. (*Steve Turner Photo*)

NEWTON ABBOT TO HEATHFIELD • **89**

NEWTON ABBOT TO ALLER JUNCTION

Newton Abbot railway station, 214 miles from London Paddington, was opened by the South Devon Railway Company in 1846. The station was originally named Newton, becoming Newton Abbot in 1877. Here, Class 47/0 47079 *G J Churchward* stands at Newton Abbot with the 1C44 13.00 Paignton to Swansea. 6 August 1983.

Above: **With the premises** of David and Charles, publishers of railway books, on the right, Class 50 50007 *Hercules* heads the 1V90 10.45 Glasgow Central to Paignton past Newton Abbot West signal box, as it departs from Newton Abbot. *Hercules* was renamed *Sir Edward Elgar* in 1984. The former diesel depot and carriage washing equipment are in the right background. 6 August 1983.

Below: **The layout was** simplified at Newton Abbot when the semaphore signals and the mechanical boxes were replaced in 1987 as part of the Exeter resignalling scheme. Here, with work progressing in the background, Class 47/4 47479 heads the 1V45 08.40 Liverpool Lime Street to Paignton away from the station. Compare this photograph with the previous one, taken five years earlier. 1 October 1988. (*Author's Collection, John Vaughan Photo*)

With power car 43125 *Merchant Venturer* leading, an InterCity 125 unit, forming a London Paddington to Penzance service, approaches Aller Junction. Note the sign on the left. The branch to Paignton left the main line to Penzance at Aller Junction, around one mile from Newton Abbot. 20 September 1985.

Opposite above: **Class 47/0 47205** heads away from Newton Abbot, towards Aller Junction, with the 1C17 08.36 Cardiff Central to Paignton. 29 June 1985.

Opposite below: **After crossing the** down line to Plymouth at Aller Junction, Class 118 DMU set P465, forming a local train from Paignton, heads for Newton Abbot. Aller Junction signal box, on the left, was closed in 1987. The lever frame is now in use in the signal box at Broadway on the Gloucestershire Warwickshire Steam Railway. 20 September 1985.

NEWTON ABBOT TO ALLER JUNCTION • 93

Above: **Class 45 'Peak'** 45117 heads the 1M22 11.28 Paignton to Manchester Piccadilly past Aller Junction. 29 June 1985.

Opposite above: **With the road** set for the Plymouth line, Class 47/0 47249 approaches the signal gantry at Aller Junction with a Severn Tunnel Junction to St Blazey Speedlink service. Three TTA china clay slurry tanks are behind an HEA hopper wagon, near the front of the train. 20 September 1985.

Opposite below: **With the signalling** control transferred to Exeter panel and the closure of Aller Junction box, a new junction was installed for the Paignton branch in 1987, about ½ mile closer to Newton Abbot. Here, Class 47/8 47853 heads the 09.30 Glasgow Central to Paignton down the Paignton line at Aller in the same location as the previous photograph. 19 June 1993.

NEWTON ABBOT TO ALLER JUNCTION • 95

ALLER JUNCTION TO PAIGNTON

Left: **Class 47/0 47274** and Class 45 45070 approach Aller Junction with the 1M65 16.08 Paignton to Liverpool Lime Street. The Class 47/0 was detached at Newton Abbot. 21 September 1985.

Opposite above: **Class 50 50005** *Collingwood* heads down the Paignton line, near Kingskerswell, with the 08.15 Basingstoke to Paignton service. The Plymouth line is in the left background. 3 September 1989.

Opposite below: **Class 45 'Peak'** 45015 heads away from Torre with the 1M65 16.08 Paignton to Liverpool Lime Street. 29 June 1985.

ALLER JUNCTION TO PAIGNTON • 97

Class 50 50032 *Courageous* passes Torre with the 1C23 09.07 London Paddington to Paignton, 'Torbay Express'. Opened in 1848 as Torquay, the station was the terminus of the line from Newton Abbot until the line was extended in 1859, when it was renamed Torre. The GWR Type 7 signal box, opened in 1922, is a Grade II listed building, as are the station buildings. 29 June 1985.

Opposite above: **Class 50 50032** *Courageous* arrives at Torquay with the 1A64 13.55 Paignton to London Paddington. The station was opened by the Dartmouth and Torbay Railway in August 1859. The Saxby & Farmer signal box, opened around 1873, was closed in 1984. The box, a listed building, still stands. 29 June 1985.

Opposite below: **Class 50 50006** *Neptune* waits to depart from Torquay with a Paignton to London Paddington service. 21 September 1985.

ALLER JUNCTION TO PAIGNTON • 99

Skipper 142 024, forming a local service from Newton Abbot to Paignton, departs from Torquay. The Class 142 Pacers were built for British Rail between 1985 and 1987. The units numbered 142 015 to 027 were painted in a GWR style chocolate and cream livery, for service in the West Country, where they were marketed as Skippers. 30 August 1987.

Opposite above: **InterCity 125 unit,** set 253 019, passes Hollicombe as it runs down the branch to Paignton. 4 April 1983.

Opposite below: **Class 108 DMU** set B962 and a second two-car set, forming the 11.00 Paignton to Newton Abbot service, are pictured near Hollicombe, heading for Torre. 3 September 1989.

ALLER JUNCTION TO PAIGNTON • 101

Above: **Class 47/4 47500** *Great Western* climbs away from Paignton with the 2B23 11.55 service to Exeter St Davids. 4 April 1983.

Below: **Class 45 'Peak'** 45070 is about to cross Torbay Road, as it arrives at its destination with the 1V71 08.20 Liverpool Lime Street to Paignton. The GWR Type 5 Paignton North signal box was opened circa 1890, replacing an earlier box, and closed in March 1988. 21 September 1985.

ALLER JUNCTION TO PLYMOUTH AND KEYHAM

Class 37/5 37674 and Class 37/4 37412 take the Plymouth line away from Aller with the 6V70 08.28 SO Bescot to St. Blazey china clay empty 'Polybulk' hoppers, a forwarding connection of 6G56, the 17:15 FO Cliffe Vale to Bescot. 25 April 1992.

Above: **Class 37/0 37207** *William Cookworthy* heads a train of five-plank vacuum-braked UCV clayhoods along the Plymouth line near Aller Junction. The train, which originated at Heathfield, is bound for Lostwithiel and Carne Point. The canvas hoods on the four-wheel wagons protected the clay and kept it dry. They were withdrawn in the late 1980s when they were replaced with modern air-braked stock. 20 September 1985.

Opposite above: **Class 50 50005** *Collingwood* heads the 1C52 14.27 London Paddington to Penzance out of Dainton Tunnel, near the summit of Dainton Bank. The main line bank, with a gradient varying between 1 in 36 and 1 in 57, is the third steepest in Britain. The Western Region Dainton Tunnel signal box, located just south of the tunnel, was opened in 1965, replacing an earlier Saxby & Farmer Type 5 box. 29 June 1985.

Opposite below: **Class 47/8 47816** heads the 1C35 11.05 London Paddington to Penzance through Totnes station. Opened by the South Devon Railway Company in 1847, Totnes became the junction for the Buckfastleigh, Totnes, and South Devon Railway's line to Ashburton in 1872. Part of the branch line has since been preserved. 26 August 1989.

ALLER JUNCTION TO PLYMOUTH AND KEYHAM • 105

Above: **Assisting an InterCity** 125 unit, forming the 1V87 12.10 Liverpool Lime Street to Penzance, Class 58 58002 rounds the curve to the west of Totnes station and begins the climb of Rattery Bank. The Class 58 was attached at Birmingham New Street. 1 September 1984.

Opposite above: **Class 37/5 diesel-electrics** 37670 and 37669 approach Totnes, at the foot of Rattery Bank, with the 6S55 Burngullow to Irvine 'Silver Bullets', loaded with china clay slurry for the Caledonian paper mill. Rattery Bank climbs for around 4¼ miles from Totnes with the gradient varying between 1 in 45 and 1 in 90. 16 July 1989.

Opposite below: **Class 47/8 47828** is pictured assisting an InterCity 125 unit at the site of the former Brent station at South Brent. The working is the 11.50 Plymouth to York. Brent station was opened by the South Devon Railway in 1848 and became the junction for the branch to Kingsbridge in 1893. The station closed in 1964. The signal box remained in use until 1973, when control passed to Plymouth power box. It was demolished in 2014. 3 September 1989.

ALLER JUNCTION TO PLYMOUTH AND KEYHAM • 107

Above: **Class 50 50028** *Tiger* passes Ivybridge with the 2C08 09.50 Plymouth to Paignton. Ivybridge station, opened in 1848, was closed to passengers in 1959, closing completely in 1965. A new station was opened by British Rail to the east of the original station in July 1994. 3 September 1989.

Opposite above: **An InterCity 125** unit, forming the 06.55 Glasgow Queen Street to Newquay service, passes Plympton signal box. Plympton station closed to passengers in 1959, but goods traffic continued until 1964. The signal box, located on the Down platform of Plympton station, remained in operation until June 1967. 26 August 1989.

Opposite below: **Class 50/1 50149** *Defiance* approaches Tavistock Junction Yard with the 10.25 Heathfield to St Blazey china clay. In 1987, 50049 was modified for use on freight trains, painted in Trainload grey livery with Railfreight decals, and renumbered 50149. Based at Plymouth Laira depot, it worked china clay trains in Devon and Cornwall. By 1989 the locomotive had returned to its former identity. 21 September 1988. (*John Whitehouse Photo*)

ALLER JUNCTION TO PLYMOUTH AND KEYHAM • 109

Class 33/0 'Cromptons' 33042 and 33064 head the 1Z34 18.10 Plymouth to London Paddington past Tavistock Junction Yard. The train ran in connection with an open day at Plymouth Laira depot. Note the withdrawn Class 50 locomotives in the background. 5 September 1991.

Opposite above: **Class 50** 50026 *Indomitable* crosses the River Plym as it heads away from Plymouth with the 2C08 09.40 Plymouth to Paignton. 5 August 1990.

Opposite below: **With 50020** *Revenge* at the front of the line, six withdrawn Class 50 diesel-electrics stand in Ocean Sidings, Plymouth. The River Plym is behind. 4 May 1991.

ALLER JUNCTION TO PLYMOUTH AND KEYHAM • 111

112 • RAILWAYS IN DEVON AND CORNWALL IN THE LATE 20TH CENTURY

Opposite above: **Class 47/8 47836** passes Laira depot with the 1M38 15.44 Plymouth to Derby, as it heads away from Plymouth. 4 May 1991.

Opposite below: **In September 1991,** an open day was held at Plymouth Laira depot, with a DMU providing a shuttle service between the depot and the station. Here, Class 101 DMU set P870 heads away from the depot, bound for Plymouth station. 15 September 1991.

With power car 43075 leading, an InterCity 125 unit forming an empty stock working from Laira depot to Plymouth station, runs alongside the River Plym. 15 September 1991.

114 • RAILWAYS IN DEVON AND CORNWALL IN THE LATE 20TH CENTURY

Opposite above: **Hunslet-Barclay Class 20/9** diesel-electrics 20901 *Nancy* and 20904 *Janis* power a weed-killing train along the Cattewater branch, Plymouth. The locomotives were previously numbered 20041 and 20101. 8 April 1990. (*Author's Collection, John Vaughan Photo*)

Opposite below: **Class 37/5 diesel-electrics** 37673 and 37671 *Tre Pol* and *Pen* stand in Plymouth Friary yard with Pathfinder Tours' 1Z18 'The Tamar Tart' from Manchester Piccadilly. 15 September 1991.

Class 47/8 47829 departs from Plymouth with the 1M48 15.44 Plymouth to Derby. Opened in 1877 as a joint station for the GWR and the LSWR, the station was originally named Plymouth North Road. The three Class 50s in the background, 50007, 50033, and 50050, were the motive power for Pathfinder Tours' 'The Cornish Caper', which ran on that day. 19 March 1994.

Class 37/5 37668 leads the returning Pathfinder Tours' 'The Pixie' through Keyham. Class 37/5 37521 is on the rear of the train. The railtour ran from Bristol Temple Meads to Calstock. Keyham station, located close to Devonport dockyard, was opened by the GWR in June 1900. 3 April 1994.

In August 1983, two Class 50 diesel-electrics were the motive power used on an excursion train from Worcester to Plymouth. Here, 50001 *Dreadnought* leads the train on to the Up line at Keyham, ready for the return journey. Class 50 50049 *Defiance* is on the rear of the train. The line to Devonport dockyard is on the left. 28 August 1983.

THE GUNNISLAKE BRANCH

Left: **The former LSWR** line to Gunnislake in Cornwall runs from Plymouth in Devon. Here, a two-car DMU, forming a Plymouth to Gunnislake service, runs under the Royal Albert Bridge on the Plymouth side of the River Tamar. 23 July 1988.

Opposite: **A two-car DMU,** forming a Gunnislake to Plymouth service, heads south, alongside the River Tamar, towards the Royal Albert Bridge. 16 July 1988.

Above: **A two-car Class** 101 DMU, forming a Gunnislake to Plymouth service, pauses at Bere Ferrers. The station, opened in June 1890, is on the former Southern Railway line between Exeter and Plymouth via Okehampton. The LSWR signal box was moved to Bere Ferrers from Pinhoe for preservation in February 1988. 16 July 1988.

Opposite above: **A two-car Class** 101 DMU, forming a Plymouth to Gunnislake service, is pictured at the Bere Alston station stop. Originally named Beer Alston, the station was opened in 1890 by the Plymouth, Devonport and South Western Junction Railway. Its name was changed to Bere Alston in 1898. It was the junction station for the lines to Tavistock and Callington via Gunnislake. The signal box, opened in 1890, was closed 1970. 16 July 1988.

Opposite below: **Pathfinder Tours'** 'The Pixie' passes Bere Alston behind Class 37/5 37521. A second Class 37/5, 37668, is on the rear of the train. The railtour ran from Bristol Temple Meads to Calstock. 3 April 1994.

THE GUNNISLAKE BRANCH • 121

A two-car DMU, forming a Gunnislake to Plymouth service, crosses the River Tamar on Calstock viaduct. The viaduct, built in 1907, has thirteen arches. It is a Grade II listed structure. A steam-powered lift was attached to the viaduct, allowing wagons to be raised and lowered from and to the quays below. The lift was taken out of use in 1934. 16 July 1988.

Gunnislake is the present-day terminus of the branch line from Plymouth. Here, a Class 117 DMU, forming a service to Plymouth, waits for its departure time at Gunnislake. This photograph, taken in the 1970s, shows the old station, opened in 1908, before the line was cut back to the other side of Station Road in 1994. The new station has a single platform with a modern waiting shelter. (*Author's Collection*)

SALTASH TO LISKEARD

Above: **An InterCity 125** unit, forming a London Paddington to Penzance service, heads away from the camera as it crosses the Royal Albert Bridge over the River Tamar and heads for Saltash in Cornwall. The bridge was designed by Isambard Kingdom Brunel and opened by Prince Albert on 2 May 1859. The Tamar road bridge is behind. 1 September 1984.

Opposite above: **This view of** the Royal Albert Bridge, over the River Tamar, shows an InterCity 125 unit, forming a Penzance to London Paddington service, heading for Plymouth in Devon. Coombe Viaduct, at Saltash in Cornwall, is in the background. 23 July 1988.

Opposite below: **Class 47/0 47128** heads the St Austell to London Paddington Motorail through Saltash which, as the sign says is the first, or in this case the last, station in Cornwall. The station was opened by the Cornwall Railway in 1859, which was amalgamated with the GWR in 1889. 1 September 1984.

SALTASH TO LISKEARD • 125

Above: **Class 50s 50008** *Thunderer* and **50015** *Valiant* trail at the rear of Pathfinder Tours' 'The Valiant Thunderer' as it passes the site of Defiance Platform, opened by the GWR in 1905 to serve the torpedo training school on HMS *Defiance*, moored at Wearde Quay. Class 50033 *Glorious* is on the front of the train. The railtour ran from Manchester Piccadilly to Newquay. 23 November 1991.

Opposite above: **Class 50 50013** *Agincourt* crosses Lynher Viaduct, over the River Lynher, with the 1E91 08.53 Penzance to Newcastle. 20 April 1985. (*Steve Turner Photo*)

Opposite below: **An InterCity 125** unit, forming a Penzance to London Paddington service, passes St Germans station. The station was opened by the Cornwall Railway in 1859. 1 September 1984.

SALTASH TO LISKEARD • **127**

Class 45 'Peak' 45002 heads an eastbound freight, bound for Severn Tunnel Junction, away from Tresulgan Viaduct, located ¾ mile east of Menheniot. The first six continental wagons contain bagged china clay for export and the rear six are empty PWA 'Palvans', returning to Ince and Elton after transporting fertilizer to UKF at Truro. 19 February 1982. (*Author's Collection, John Vaughan Photo*)

Opposite above: **Class 47/4 47443** passes Menheniot with the 1E18 12.20 Newquay to Leeds. The station was opened by the Cornwall Railway in 1859. The GWR signal box, opened in 1892 replacing an earlier box, was closed in 1973. 1 September 1984.

Opposite below: **With power car** 43186 leading, an InterCity 125 unit heads west after crossing Bolitho Viaduct. The eight span viaduct, located ¼ mile east of Liskeard, was built in 1882. 20 October 1988. (*Author's Collection, John Vaughan Photo*)

Class 45 'Peak' 45005 approaches Liskeard with the 1V76 09.36 Liverpool Lime Street to Penzance. The line on the left, opposite the GWR Type 27c signal box, joins the Looe to Moorswater line at Coombe. 31 August 1984.

LISKEARD TO LOOE

Passengers are waiting as Class 117 DMU set B450 arrives at the platform for Looe at Liskeard station. Opened in 1859, the station is approximately 18 miles west of Plymouth. It is the junction for the Looe Valley Line, the platform for Looe being at right angles to the main line. Trains to Looe first run northwards before swinging round towards the south and descending the steep gradient to pass under Liskeard Viaduct, east of the station. They then reverse at Coombe Junction. 25 August 1984.

Above: **Class 37/4 37412** approaches Coombe Junction with a train of loaded CDA hopper wagons from Moorswater clay dries, bound for Carne Point, Fowey. Because of the steep gradient up to Liskeard, the number of loaded wagons was limited, so a few trips would have to be made before a full train could be assembled. Coombe Junction halt is in the background and the junction itself is behind the photographer, with the line to Liskeard forking to the left. Moorswater Viaduct is beyond Coombe Junction halt, in the background. 27 May 1993. (*David Rostance Photo*)

Opposite: **After passing under** Moorswater Viaduct, Class 37/5 37521 heads a train of loaded CDA hopper wagons towards Coombe Junction and Liskeard. The 45-ton four-wheel covered CDA wagon, based on the HAA coal hopper wagon, was introduced in 1987 for the English China Clay traffic in Cornwall. A total of 140 were built, 16 of which were converted from HAA hopper wagons, including prototype number 353224. August 2023 saw the end of the CDA wagons on local china clay traffic, around thirty-five years after replacing the clayhoods. 27 August 1996. (*Steve Widdowson Photo*)

Class 118 DMU set P465, forming a Looe to Liskeard service, heads away from Coombe Junction halt. The Liskeard and Looe Railway was opened in 1860 for goods traffic and for passengers in 1879. An extension from Coombe Junction to Liskeard was opened in 1901. 1 September 1984.

Class 118 DMU set P465, forming a Looe to Liskeard service, arrives at St Keyne halt. The halt opened in 1902. 1 September 1984.

Above: **Pressed Steel Class** 121 railcar W55025, forming a Looe to Liskeard service, arrives at Sandplace. The station, opened in 1881, is 6½ miles south of Liskeard. 31 August 1984.

Below: **Class 121 railcar** W55032 waits at Looe, ready to depart as the 08.32 to Liskeard. The original Looe station, opened in 1879, was replaced in 1968 when the line was cut back by 110 yards. 20 April 1985. (*Steve Turner Photo*)

LISKEARD TO BODMIN PARKWAY

On a very wet day, Class 37/0 37281 arrives at Liskeard with a train of clayhoods from Moorswater clay dries. The train is bound for Lostwithiel for onward movement to Carne Point, Fowey. 26 September 1984. (*Steve Turner Photo*)

138 • RAILWAYS IN DEVON AND CORNWALL IN THE LATE 20TH CENTURY

Opposite above: **Class 47/0 47128** crosses Moorswater Viaduct with the 1M76 08.55 Newquay to Manchester Piccadilly. The eight-arch stone viaduct was built in 1881, replacing an earlier structure. Some of the piers of the original viaduct still remain and one can be seen here, alongside the new viaduct. The former Liskeard and Looe Railway is in the foreground. 1 September 1984.

Opposite below: **Viewed from the** north side of the line, Class 45 'Peak' 45015 heads the 1C82 13.54 Penzance to Bristol Temple Meads eastwards over Moorswater Viaduct. The viaduct and the remaining piers of the original structure were listed Grade II in 1985. 31 August 1984.

Below: **In this 1979** photograph, an unidentified Class 50 heads an eastbound express over Penadlake Viaduct, 1¾ miles east of Bodmin Road. The viaduct was built in 1877, replacing an earlier viaduct. (*Author's Collection, John Vaughan Photo*)

Above: **Class 50 50046** *Ajax* starts the 1O86 10.50 Penzance to Brighton away from the Bodmin Parkway station stop. The station, situated 3 miles from the town of Bodmin, was opened in June 1859 as Bodmin Road. It was renamed Bodmin Parkway in November 1983. The signal box, on the down platform beyond the footbridge, is a GWR Type 3 design. After closure in May 1985, it was reopened as a café. 25 August 1984.

Opposite: **An InterCity 125** unit, forming a London Paddington to Penzance service, departs from Bodmin Parkway. The wooden station buildings were replaced with brick buildings in 1989. 25 August 1984.

BODMIN PARKWAY TO WENFORD BRIDGE

In 1887, the GWR opened a line from Bodmin Road to Boscarne Junction, on the LSWR line from Padstow to Bodmin which had a branch to Wenford. The former LSWR Bodmin station was renamed Bodmin General in 1949. The line lost its passenger service in 1967, but goods traffic continued until November 1983. In 1990, the line was reopened as a heritage railway by the Bodmin and Wenford Railway. Here, Class 37/0 37142 is pictured at Bodmin General station, running round F & W Railtours' 'Pixielated Pixie', en route from Boscarne Junction to Cheltenham Spa. 17 August 1980. (*Steve Turner Photo*)

Class 08 diesel-electric shunter 08091 heads a loaded china clay train to Bodmin Road away from Bodmin General. December 1979. (*Author's Collection, John Vaughan Photo*)

A suitably rusty and weathered St Blazey Class 08 shunter, 08488, waits at Stannon clay dries to work the next trip of loaded china clay wagons along the Wenford Bridge to Boscarne Junction mineral line. From there the wagons will be taken onward via Bodmin by a Class 37 locomotive. 24 June 1983. (*Don Gatehouse Photo*)

Opposite: **Class 37/0** 37185 has arrived at Boscarne Junction with a train of twenty empty OOV clayhoods for onward delivery to Stannon clay dries on the Wenford Bridge line using Class 08 haulage. The Bodmin and Wenford Railway opened a station here in 1996 and added a stone-built waiting room in 2010. This station is served from Bodmin General and is adjacent to the Camel Trail, the footpath and cycle route to Wadebridge, Padstow, and Bodmin. 27 June 1983. (*Don Gatehouse Photo*)

LOSTWITHIEL TO CARNE POINT

Above: **Class 45 'Peak'** 45019 heads a short train of empty PCA cement tanks from the Blue Circle cement terminal at Chacewater through Lostwithiel. The tank wagons will go forward in a St Blazey to Severn Tunnel Junction Speedlink service. The Chacewater traffic ended in 1987. 31 August 1984.

Opposite above: **Class 37/0 37247** runs alongside the River Fowey, near Lostwithiel, as it heads a train of loaded clayhoods to Carne Point, Fowey. 31 August 1984.

Opposite below: **Class 37/0 37247** passes Golant harbour with a china clay train, bound for Carne Point. 31 August 1984.

LOSTWITHIEL TO CARNE POINT • 147

Above: **Class 37/0 37181,** seen from an elevated viewpoint, heads south past Golant with a train of clayhoods. The River Fowey estuary is behind. 28 September 1984. (*Steve Turner Photo*)

Below: **China clay is** shipped all over the world from Carne Point. Here, after unloading at English China Clays' facility at Carne Point, next to the River Fowey, Class 37/5 37674 prepares to depart with its train of empty clayhoods, bound for Goonbarrow. 25 August 1987. (*John Whiteley Photo*)

LOSTWITHIEL TO PAR

Class 37/0 37207 *William Cookworthy* approaches Lostwithiel with 6B48 18.30 Plymouth Friary to St Blazey cement tanks. The name *William Cookworthy*, an English Quaker minister who established the Plymouth China factory, was carried by both 37207 and 37675, previously numbered 37164. 19 April 1985. (*Steve Turner Photo*)

Constructed in 1981, Class 140 001 was the prototype Pacer DMU. In the 1980s, this, the only member of the class, was used as a demonstration unit. Here the unit is pictured heading south, as it approaches Lostwithiel station. It is now preserved at the Keith and Dufftown Railway. 29 August 1984.

Opposite above: Class 37/5 diesel-electrics 37675 *William Cookworthy* and 37679 head a St Blazey to Exeter freight away from Lostwithiel. The former GWR Lostwithiel Crossing signal box, opened in 1893, stands at the northern end of platform 1. The Type 5 box is a Grade II listed building. 25 July 1988.

Opposite below: Class 37/5 37672 *Freight Transport Association* departs from Lostwithiel with a train of empty CDA china clay hoppers, bound for Goonbarrow. 25 July 1988.

Class 37/0 37207 *William Cookworthy* shunts clayhoods at Lostwithiel. 31 August 1984.

Opposite above: **Class 45 'Peak'** 45134 arrives at Lostwithiel with the 1E25 09.18 Penzance to Leeds. The station was opened by the Cornwall Railway in 1859. 31 August 1984.

Opposite below: **Class 50 50019** *Ramillies* heads the 11.50 Penzance to Plymouth empty stock out of Treverrin Tunnel. Located between Lostwithiel and Par, the tunnel is 565 yards long. 28 September 1984. (*Steve Turner Photo*)

LOSTWITHIEL TO PAR • 153

Class 37/5 37669 heads west through Par station with a single clay slurry tank. 26 July 1988.

Opposite above: **Class 45 'Peak'** 45017 arrives at Par with the 1C82 13.54 Penzance to Bristol Temple Meads. Par signal box, a GWR Type 2 design opened in 1879, is a Grade II listed building. The lines on the right run to St Blazey and Newquay. 29 August 1984.

Opposite below: **Class 45 'Peak'** 45072 heads a St Blazey to Severn Tunnel Junction Speedlink past Par. In the consist are vans, TTA tank wagons and PCA cement tanks. On the left, Class 118 DMU set P464 stands in the platform waiting to depart to Newquay. An inspector's saloon is in the siding on the right. 29 August 1984.

LOSTWITHIEL TO PAR • 155

Class 37/0 37207 *William Cookworthy* takes the line to St Blazey and Newquay, as it approaches Par with a train of empty clayhoods. 29 August 1984.

Before the introduction of cast diamond-shaped Railfreight depot plaques in the late 1980s, a number of Class 37 diesel-electrics carried a Cornish Railways 'Lizzie the Lizard' logo. This example, on the bodyside of 37181, was photographed at Par. The later cast depot plaque for St Blazey illustrated a lizard. 31 August 1984.

PAR TO NEWQUAY

Class 118 DMU set P461, forming a Par to Newquay service, heads away from Par and approaches Middleway Crossing. A line of UCV clayhoods, without their canvas covers, stands in St Blazey yard in the background. 29 August 1984.

Above: **Class 08 diesel-electric** shunter 08801 approaches Middleway Crossing with a VGA van containing bagged clay from Pontsmill dries. The signals indicate that the train is bound for St Blazey yard. 29 August 1984.

Opposite above: **Class 37/5 37675** *William Cookworthy* stands in St Blazey yard with a train of china clay 'Tigers'. St Blazey signal box, a GWR Type 7 box opened in 1908, is in the background. 10 June 1987. (*Author's Collection, John Vaughan Photo*)

Opposite below: **Class 37/0 37207** *William Cookworthy* and Class 47/0 47199 stand at St Blazey locomotive depot. Opened in 1874, it was built as the headquarters of the Cornwall Minerals Railway and was originally named Par. Amongst the buildings was a roundhouse with nine roads around a turntable. The roundhouse has since been converted into industrial units. 19 April 1985. (*Steve Turner Photo*)

PAR TO NEWQUAY • 159

Above: **Viewed from Treffry** Viaduct, Class 46 'Peak' 46009 heads south with a train from Newquay. Treffry Viaduct, located near Luxulyan, is a railway viaduct and aqueduct. Completed in 1844, the viaduct once carried a tramway across the valley. 21 September 1979. (*Author's Collection, John Vaughan Photo*)

Opposite above: **Class 118 DMU** set P460, forming a Newquay to Par service, departs from Luxulyan. The station was opened by the Cornwall Minerals Railway in 1876. 28 August 1984.

Opposite below: **The shunter waits** as Class 37/0 diesel-electrics 37247 and 37181 arrive at Goonbarrow Junction with a train of empty clayhoods from Fowey Docks. Goonbarrow Junction signal box is a GWR Type 7d design, opened circa 1909 to replace an earlier box. 19 April 1985. (*Steve Turner Photo*)

PAR TO NEWQUAY • 161

Above: **Class 37/5 37673,** on the north end of the train, leads Pathfinder Tours' 'Cornish Centurion 2' from Manchester Piccadilly into Bugle station, before heading back to Par. Class 50 diesel-electrics 50015 *Valiant* and 50008 *Thunderer* are on the rear of the train. The station was opened by the Cornwall Minerals Railway in 1876. The branch line, serving English China Clay at Carbis Wharf, diverged from the Newquay line at Goonbarrow Junction, to the south of Bugle. The branch closed in 1989 leaving only a single track through the station. 4 May 1991.

Opposite above: **Token duties are** carried out as 50044 *Exeter* pauses at St Dennis Junction, next to the GWR signal box, with the 16.20 Plymouth to Newquay. This was the junction for the line to English China Clay at Meledor Mill, closed in the early 1980s. 30 August 1984.

Opposite below: **An InterCity 125** unit, with power cars 43143 and 43105, stands at Newquay station between duties. The station, just over 302 miles from London Paddington, was opened in 1876 by the Cornwall Minerals Railway. Purchased by the GWR in 1896, it was reduced to one platform in 1987. 10 June 1989. (*Author's Collection, John Vaughan Photo*)

PAR TO NEWQUAY • 163

Class 108 DMU set 862 stands at the end of the line at Newquay station. The DMU will later form a service to Par. 9 June 1989. (*Author's Collection, John Vaughan Photo*)

ST AUSTELL TO BURNGULLOW INCLUDING THE FREIGHT LINE FROM BURNGULLOW JUNCTION

Class 45 'Peak' 45139 departs from St Austell with the 1V76 09.36 Liverpool Lime Street to Penzance. The Grade II listed station was opened by the Cornwall Railway in May 1859. 27 August 1984.

Class 50 50010 *Monarch* arrives at St Austell with the 08.53 Penzance to Newcastle. The GWR St Austell signal box was closed in 1980 when control was transferred to Par. 28 August 1984.

Opposite above: Viewed from the footbridge next to the signal box, Class 45 'Peak' 45139 approaches St Austell station with the 1E25 09.18 Penzance to Leeds. 28 August 1984.

Opposite below: In this 1982 photograph, InterCity 125 unit 253 038 climbs the gradient from St Austell as it heads west to Penzance. The disused Trenance dries are on the left. (*Author's Collection, John Vaughan Photo*)

ST AUSTELL TO BURNGULLOW INCLUDING THE FREIGHT LINE • 167

Above: **Class 45 'Peak'** 45015 passes Burngullow with the 07.50 Bristol Temple Meads to Penzance. Blackpool clay works is on the left, alongside the main line. 30 August 1984.

Opposite above: **Class 37/0 37247** heads a trip freight from the Parkandillack line on to the main line at Burngullow. The train is made up of a van containing bagged clay, two hopper wagons, and two PBA 'Tigers'. The wagons will go forward on a St Blazey to Severn Tunnel Junction Speedlink service. 25 July 1988.

Opposite below: **What is now** the freight line from Burngullow to Parkandillack, serving various china clay works, was opened in 1869 by the Newquay and Cornwall Junction Railway. In 1874, it was taken over by the Cornwall Minerals Railway, becoming part of the GWR in 1896. Here, Class 45 'Peak' 45051 pauses at Drinnick Mill goods office with a trip freight from St Blazey to Parkandillack. 19 April 1985. (*Steve Turner Photo*)

ST AUSTELL TO BURNGULLOW INCLUDING THE FREIGHT LINE • 169

Above: **Class 37/0 diesel-electrics** 37247 and 37181 approach Treviscoe with a Fowey, Carne Point to Parkandillack empty china clay working. 19 April 1985. (*Steve Turner Photo*)

Below: **Class 45 'Peak'** 45051 departs from Parkandillack china clay works with a trip freight to St Blazey Sorting Sidings. The train is made up of an HEA hopper wagon and three PBA 'Tigers'. 19 April 1985. (*Steve Turner Photo*)

BURNGULLOW JUNCTION TO TRURO

Class 47/4 47508 *Great Britain* heads the Penzance to Glasgow parcels past Burngullow Junction. The train will be divided at Bristol, with one section continuing to London Paddington. Burngullow station was closed in 1931 and the signal box in 1986, when the Burngullow to Probus section of the main line was singled. The signals were then controlled from Par. 30 August 1984.

Above: **Class 47/4 47511** approaches Truro with the 1C47 14.15 London Paddington to Penzance. Truro signal box, opened as Truro East in 1899, is a GWR Type 7A box. 25 August 1984.

Below: **Class 50 50036** *Victorious* arrives at Truro with the 1S71 07.30 Penzance to Aberdeen. The station was opened by the Cornwall Railway in 1859. 28 August 1984.

TRURO TO FALMOUTH

The Falmouth line diverges from the main line to Penzance at Penwithers Junction, west of Truro. The line passes over a number of viaducts as it passes through the Cornish countryside, the first of which is Carnon Viaduct. Here, Class 118 DMU set P470 approaches the viaduct as it heads for Falmouth. The nine-arch viaduct was opened in June 1933, replacing an earlier structure. 23 February 1982. (*Author's Collection, John Vaughan Photo*)

Above: **Sprinters 153 382 and 150 230**, forming a Truro to Falmouth service, arrive at Penmere, located in the eastern part of Falmouth and 2 miles from Falmouth Docks station. The station was opened by the GWR in July 1925. 31 July 1993. (*Steve Widdowson Photo*)

Opposite above: **Class 33 'Cromptons'** 33050 *Isle of Grain* and 33063 arrive at Falmouth Docks with Merlin Railtours' the 'Cornish Construction Crompton' from Basingstoke. Class 37/5 37675 is on the rear of the train. Falmouth Docks station, the terminus of the line from Penwithers Junction, was opened in 1863 as Falmouth. It was closed in 1970 but was reopened in 1975 and renamed Falmouth Docks in 1989. 21 March 1992. (*Steve Widdowson Photo*)

Opposite below: **Class 121 DMU** W55009 stands at Falmouth station, after arriving from Truro. The station, near Carrick Roads and Falmouth Bay and almost in the shadow of Pendennis Castle, was renamed Falmouth Docks the following year. 22 October 1988. (*Author's Collection, John Vaughan Photo*)

TRURO TO ST ERTH

Above: **With the remains** of one of the two former engine houses at Hallenbeagle copper mine on the left, Class 155 Super Sprinter 155 301, forming the 13.30 Penzance to Plymouth service, heads east towards Truro at Scorrier, between Redruth and Truro. The engine house dates from 1864. 4 May 1991.

Opposite above: **An InterCity 125** unit, forming a Penzance to Paddington service, passes Drump Lane signal box. The GWR Type 7d box, located east of Redruth station, was opened in December 1911. The former Redruth goods yard, opened in 1912, is on the left. 27 August 1984.

Opposite below: **Class 47/0 47190** arrives at Redruth with the 07.50 Bristol Temple Meads to Penzance. Redruth station is located between Truro and Camborne. The main station building was built by the GWR in the 1930s but an earlier wooden building remains on the Down platform. 27 August 1984.

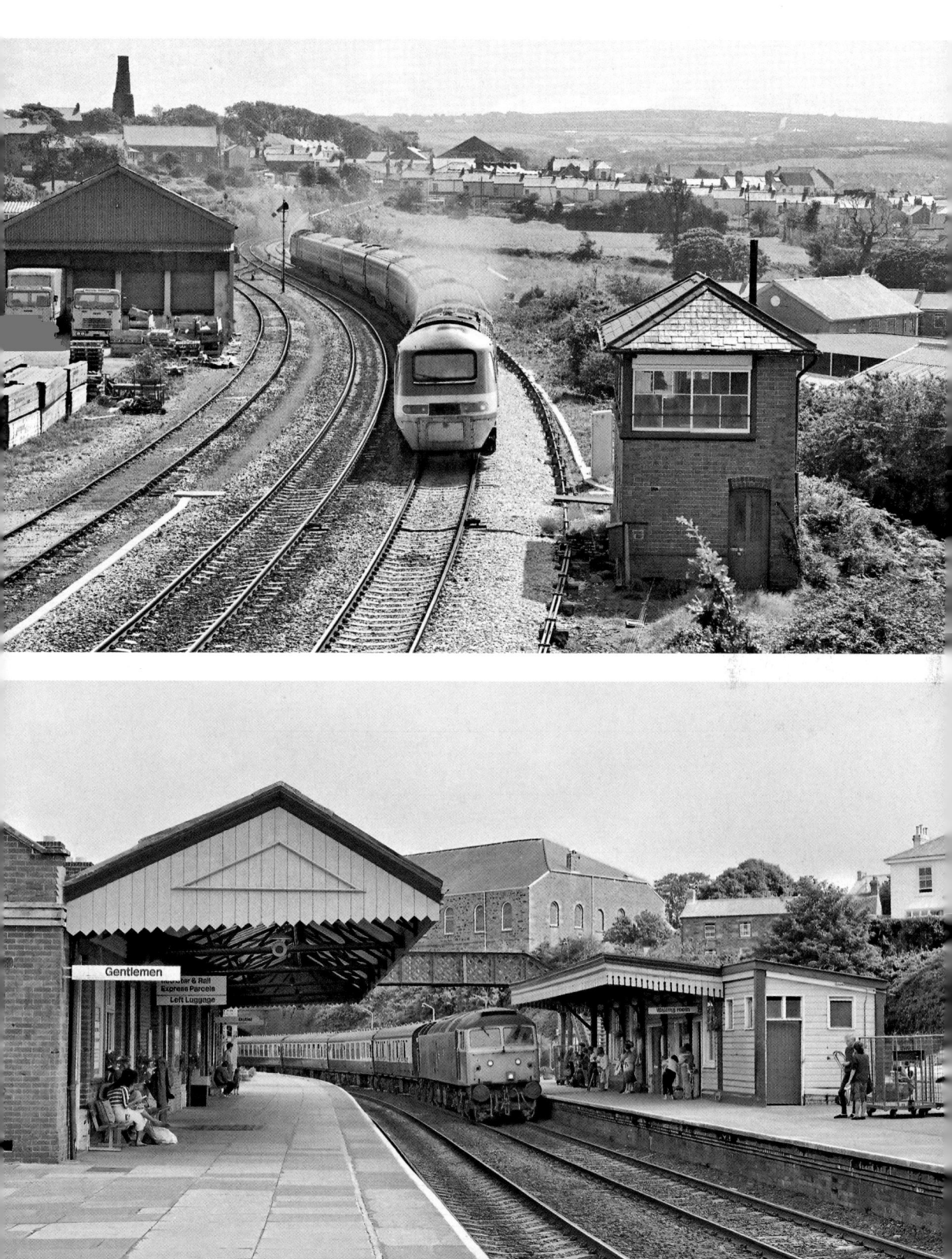

Above: **With mines and** engine houses all around, Class 50 diesel-electrics 50015 *Valiant* and 50008 *Thunderer* head west past the site of Carn Brea station, closed in 1961, with Pathfinder Tours' 'Cornish Centurion 2' from Manchester Piccadilly to Penzance. 4 May 1991.

Opposite above: **Class 50 50050** *Fearless* arrives at Camborne with the 1A83 10.45 Penzance to London Paddington. The station was opened by the Hayle Railway in 1843. 23 September 1983. (*John Whitehouse Photo*)

Opposite below: **Class 45 'Peak'** 45138 heads the 1C11 06.50 Swindon to Penzance over Angarrack Viaduct. The eleven-arch viaduct crosses the Angarrack River between Camborne and Hayle. 7 June 1985. (*Steve Turner Photo*)

Above: **After running round** its train at St Erth, Class 50 50004 *St Vincent* heads east, near Copperhouse, with a freight from Chacewater cement terminal to St Blazey. The Blue Circle cement terminal at Chacewater was located between Redruth and Truro. 6 June 1985. (*Steve Turner Photo*)

Opposite above: **Class 50 50016** *Barham* heads the 07.02 Exeter St Davids to Penzance over Guildford Viaduct. The viaduct crosses Guildford Road and the Hayle Bypass to the east of Hayle station. 5 June 1985. (*Steve Turner Photo*)

Opposite below: **After crossing Hayle** Viaduct to the west of the station, 50024 *Vanguard* arrives at Hayle with the 09.32 Penzance to London Paddington. The station was opened by the West Cornwall Railway in 1852. 7 June 1985. (*Steve Turner Photo*)

Above: **With Copperhouse Pool** in the foreground, a two-car Super Sprinter, forming a Plymouth to Penzance service, heads away from Hayle and crosses Hayle Viaduct. The viaduct, built by the GWR in 1886, replaced Brunel's original viaduct of 1852. 30 July 1988.

Below: **After visiting Chacewater** cement terminal, Class 47/4 47091 *Thor* nears St Erth with a trip freight from St Blazey. A fuel tank for Penzance TMD is on the rear of the train. 3 June 1985. (*Steve Turner Photo*)

Above: **Class 45 'Peak'** 45107 approaches St Erth with the 07.00 Exeter St Davids to Penzance. The signal box was opened in 1899, replacing an earlier box. 27 August 1984.

Below: **An unidentified Class 47** arrives at St Erth with an eastbound extra. The station, opened as St Ives Road by the West Cornwall Railway in 1852, was renamed St Erth in 1877 when the St Ives branch was opened. 26 August 1984.

ST ERTH TO ST IVES

Above: **Class 118 DMU** set P470, forming a service from St Ives, arrives at St Erth. 26 August 1984.

Opposite above: **Class 118 DMU** set P470, forming a St Erth to St Ives service, runs alongside the River Hayle at Lelant Saltings. 26 August 1984.

Opposite below: **Class 121 railcar** W55025, with Class 118 DMU set P470 behind, arrives at St Ives. The train is a branch line working from St Erth. 26 August 1984.

After arriving at St Ives, Class 118 DMU set P470, with Class 121 railcar W55025 behind, waits for passengers to disembark before returning to St Erth. The station, 4¼ miles from St Erth, was opened in 1877 to serve the holiday town of St Ives on the Cornish coast. 26 August 1984.

ST ERTH TO PENZANCE

Class 47/4 47656 waits for the road at Marazion with the 10.24 Penzance to Liverpool Lime Street. Marazion station, opened by the West Cornwall Railway in 1852, was closed in 1964. Note the Pullman coaches on the left, which were used for holiday accommodation. 30 July 1988.

***Above*:** **With a DMU** and a class 50 stabled with its stock on the right, Class 47/4 47615 passes Penzance signal box, as it arrives at its destination with the 2C68 09.20 Exeter St Davids to Penzance. The GWR signal box was built in 1938, replacing an earlier box. 26 August 1984.

***Opposite above*:** **Class 50 50036** *Victorious* departs from Penzance with the 1S71 07.30 Penzance to Aberdeen at the start of Britain's longest train journey. The train is due to arrive at Aberdeen at 21.40, a journey time of fourteen hours and ten minutes. The Class 50 will be replaced by an electric locomotive at Birmingham New Street. 27 August 1984.

***Opposite below*:** **Two InterCity 125** units wait for their departure times at Penzance. The station is the terminus of the main line from Plymouth and beyond, just under 327 miles from London Paddington. Opened in 1852, the station was rebuilt by the GWR in 1876 and again in the 1930s. 26 August 1984.

ST ERTH TO PENZANCE • 189

Above: **Class 50 diesel-electrics** 50017 *Royal Oak* and 50048 *Dauntless* rest between duties at Penzance. A third Class 50, 50045 *Achilles*, is on the right. 27 August 1984.

Below: **Class 33/2 'Cromptons'** 33207 and 33211 stand at the end of the line at Penzance after arriving with 'The Crompton Cornish Farewell' from London Waterloo. The railtour was organised by Network SouthEast (Salisbury). 22 October 1988. (*Author's Collection, John Vaughan Photo*)

STEAM ON THE MAIN LINE IN 1985

To celebrate the 150th Anniversary of the GWR in 1985, a series of special trains were run in the West Country using former GWR locomotives.

Here, Castle Class 4-6-0 5051 *Drysllwyn Castle* and Hall Class 4-6-0 4930 *Hagley Hall* head the 'Great Western Limited' to Bristol Temple Meads through Tiverton Junction station. The Collett Castle was built at Swindon Works in May 1936 and withdrawn from service in May 1963 when it was sold to Woodham Brothers. It was the fourth locomotive to be removed from the scrapyard for preservation and is based at Didcot Railway Centre. *Hagley Hall*, built at Swindon in 1929, is a GWR Collett Hall Class locomotive. It is one of 258 built between 1928 and 1943. Withdrawn from service in December 1963, it arrived at Barry Scrapyard in May 1964. Purchased for use on the SVR, it reached there in January 1973. 14 July 1985.

Above: **Castle Class 4-6-0s** 5051 *Drysllwyn Castle* and 7029 *Clun Castle* attract little attention as they lead a support coach along the sea wall at Teignmouth before heading a 'Great Western Limited' railtour from Plymouth to Bristol Temple Meads. *Clun Castle*, built by British Railways at Swindon Works in May 1950 to a GWR design, was fitted with a double chimney and a four-row superheater in October 1959. In 1966, it was sold to Patrick Whitehouse, its ownership later passing to 7029 Clun Castle Ltd. It is now based at Tyseley Locomotive Works. 1 September 1985.

Opposite above: **A week later** and in contrast to the previous picture, the crowds are out at Teignmouth to see 5051 *Drysllwyn Castle* and 7029 *Clun Castle* round the curve from Teignmouth station on to the sea wall with the 'Great Western Limited' to Bristol Temple Meads. 8 September 1985.

Opposite below: **Castle Class 4-6-0s** 5051 *Drysllwyn Castle* and 7029 *Clun Castle* pass Tavistock Junction Yard, as they head away from Plymouth with the 'Great Western Limited' to Bristol Temple Meads. 1 September 1985.

STEAM ON THE MAIN LINE IN 1985 • 193

PRESERVED RAILWAYS

Finally, we briefly look at some of the principal preservation operations that were active during the time period covered in this book.

The Dart Valley Railway

***Opposite*: The railway, opened** in 1969, was renamed the South Devon Railway in 1991. It initially operated from Ashburton, but currently runs for just under 7 miles from its headquarters at Buckfastleigh to a new station at Totnes Riverside. Here, GWR Collett 1400 class 0-4-2T 1450, with a Devon Belle observation car at the front of the train, runs alongside the River Dart towards Staverton. The locomotive was built at Swindon in 1935 and withdrawn from service in May 1965. 30 March 1975.

Standing in the Dart Valley Railway's locomotive depot at Buckfastleigh are GWR Collett 1366 Class 0-6-0PT 1369 and Hunslet Austerity 0-6-0ST 1004 *Glendower*. Built at Swindon in 1934, 1369's final duties were on the Bodmin and Wadebridge Railway to Wenford Bridge, where it, 1367 and 1368 replaced the Beattie well tanks which were used previously. After withdrawal in 1964, 1369 left Wadebridge under its own steam for the Dart Valley Railway. *Glendower* (3810 of 1954) was named by the National Coal Board. It was used at a number of collieries before being withdrawn at Hafodyrynys in Monmouthshire in 1973. Arriving at the Dart Valley Railway in 1978, it is currently in store. 28 August 1981.

The Torbay Steam Railway

Manor Class 4-6-0 7827 *Lydham Manor* climbs Goodrington bank, as it heads its train away from Paignton. Opened in January 1973 by the Dart Valley Light Railway Ltd, and now known as the Dartmouth Steam Railway, the railway runs for just under 7 miles along the former GWR line from Paignton to Kingswear. The Manor, built by British Railways in 1950 at Swindon Works to a GWR design, was withdrawn in October 1965 when it was acquired by Woodham Brothers. Sold to the Dart Valley Railway, it left the scrapyard in June 1970 as the fifth departure from Barry. 13 April 1974.

In December 1991, the Devon Diesel Society purchased Class 50 50002 *Superb*, initially for use on the Paignton and Dartmouth Railway, as the Torbay Steam Railway was then known. The first passenger trains hauled by 50002 ran in April 1992 and were for members and shareholders only, but although I had tickets, I chose to photograph the trains instead of riding on them. Here, *Superb* passes Goodrington Sands signal box on the Paignton and Dartmouth Railway, as it heads away from Paignton with one of the special trains. The GWR Type 28b signal box was opened in July 1928 and closed in November 1972. 25 April 1992.

The Seaton Tramway

Opposite: **The Seaton Tramway,** initially opened in 1970 and progressively extended, is a 2ft 9in gauge electric tramway which runs for 3 miles from Seaton to Colyton on the trackbed of the former branch line from Seaton Junction. Here tram car 6 waits at Colyton for its departure time to Seaton. 1 September 1989.

The Bodmin and Wenford Railway

The Bodmin and Wenford Railway runs for just over 6 miles from Bodmin Parkway to Boscarne Junction. The original line was opened in 1887 and closed in 1983. Heritage trains to Bodmin Parkway commenced in 1990 and services to Boscarne Junction began in 1996. Here, Class 50 50042 *Triumph* stands at Bodmin General with a train to Boscarne Junction. An 0-6-0 diesel-electric shunter is alongside with a Class 108 DMU on the right. The signal box is a replacement for the original, which was demolished in the late 1970s. 15 August 1998. (*John Whitehouse Photo.*)

Bagnall 0-4-0ST *Alfred* (3058 of 1953), built for use at Par Docks, stands at Bodmin General with a brake van. Short train rides from the station commenced in July 1989 and continued until services to Bodmin Parkway started in June 1990, following the granting of a light railway order in August 1989. 31 July 1989. (*Steve Widdowson Photo*)

Launceston Steam Railway

The Launceston Steam Railway is a 1ft 11½in narrow gauge railway which runs from Launceston to Newmills in Cornwall. Opened in 1983, it runs for 2½ miles along the trackbed of the former North Cornwall Railway. Here, photographed in more recent years, Hunslet Port Class 0-4-0ST *Covertcoat* (679 of 1898) stands at Newmills station with a train to Launceston. 20 August 2008.

The Plym Valley Railway

A more recent addition to the operational preserved railways of Devon and Cornwall is the Plym Valley Railway. The railway opened a new station at Marsh Mills in 1988 and trains now run from there for a little over a mile along the route of the former South Devon and Tavistock Railway, opened in 1859 and closed in 1962, to a new platform at Plym Bridge. Here, Pacer 142 023 stands at Plym Bridge station, waiting for its departure time to Marsh Mills. 2 July 2023.

BIBLIOGRAPHY

Baker, S. K., *Rail Atlas Great Britain and Ireland*, Haynes Publishing Group, 1980 and 1988
British Rail, *British Rail Passenger Timetable(s)*, May 1984-October 1993, British Railways Board, 1984-1993
British Railways Pre-Grouping Atlas and Gazetteer, Ian Allan Publishing Ltd, 1980
Cooke, R.A., *Atlas of the Great Western Railway, 1947*, Wild Swan Publications Ltd, 1988
Gradients of the British Main Line Railways, Ian Allan Publishing Ltd, 2016
Jowett, A., *Jowett's Railway Atlas of Great Britain and Ireland*, Patrick Stephens Ltd, 1989
Marsden, C., *35 Years of Main Line Diesel Traction*, Oxford Publishing Co., 1982
Rhodes, M. and Shannon, P., *Freight Only Volume 2: Southern and Central England*, Silver Link 1988
Signalling Study Group, *The Signal Box, A Pictorial History*, Oxford Publishing Co., 1986
Thomas, D. St John, *A Regional History of the Railways of Great Britain, The West Country*, David and Charles Ltd, 1960
Vaughan, J, *Diesels in the Duchy*, Ian Allan Publishing Ltd, 1983
Wood, R., *British Rail Locomotives*, Ian Allan Ltd, 1986

INDEX TO LOCATIONS (BY PAGE NUMBER)

Aller Junction 92-96, 103-104
Angarrack Viaduct 179
Axminster 61

Barnstaple 34
Bere Alston 121
Bere Ferrers 120
Blackboy Tunnel 49
Bodmin General 142-143, 199-200
Bodmin Parkway 140-141
Bolitho Viaduct 129
Boscarne Junction 144
Broadclyst 53
Buckfastleigh 195
Bugle 162
Burngullow 168-169, 171

Calstock 122
Camborne 179
Carn Brea 178
Carne Point 148
Carnon Viaduct 173
Chapelton 33
Cockwood Harbour 72
Colyton 198
Coombe Junction 132-134
Copperhouse 180
Copplestone 30

Cowley Bridge Junction 21-22, 38
Crediton 24-25
Cullompton 17

Dainton Tunnel 105
Dawlish Warren 73-74
Dawlish 75-79
Defiance Platform 126
Drinnick Mill 169
Drump Lane 177

Eggesford 31
Exeter Central 45-47
Exeter St Davids 39-45
Exminster 67-69
Exmouth Junction 50-51
Exmouth 66

Falmouth 174-175
Feniton 56

Golant 147-148
Goodrington 196-197
Goonbarrow Junction 161
Guildford Viaduct 181
Gunnislake 123

Hallenbeagle 176
Hayle 181-182

INDEX TO LOCATIONS (BY PAGE NUMBER) • 205

Heathfield 89
Hele and Bradninch 18-19
Hollicombe 101
Honiton 57

Ivybridge 108

Keyham 116-117
King's Nympton 32
Kingskerswell 97

Lapford 31
Lelant Saltings 185
Liskeard 130-131, 137
Looe 136
Lostwithiel 146-147, 149-153
Luxulyan 161
Lympstone 65
Lynher Viaduct 127

Marazion 187
Meeth 37
Meldon Quarry 29
Menheniot 129
Middleway Crossing 157-158
Moorswater Viaduct 138

New Mills 201
Newquay 163-164
Newton Abbot 85-88, 90-91
Newton St Cyres 23-24

Okehampton 27-28

Paignton 102
Par 154-156
Parkandillack 170
Parson's Tunnel 81
Penadlake Viaduct 139
Penmere 174
Penzance 188-190

Pinhoe 51-53
Plym Bridge 202
Plymouth 111-115, 118-119
Plympton 109
Polsoe Bridge 63

Redruth 177

Saltash 124-125
Sandplace 136
Seaton Junction 59
Shaldon Bridge 84-85
Shell Cove 80
St Austell 165-167
St Blazey 159
St Dennis Junction 163
St Erth 182-184
St Germans 127
St Ives 185-186
St James Park 48
St Keyne 135
Stannon Clay Dries 145
Starcross 70-71
Staverton 194
Stoke Canon 19-20

Talaton 55
Taunton 11
Tavistock Junction Yard 109-110, 193
Teignbridge 89
Teignmouth 82-84, 192-193
Tiverton Junction 13-15, 191
Tiverton Parkway 16
Topsham 64
Torquay 99-100
Torre 97-98
Torrington 35-36
Totnes 105-107

Treffry Viaduct 160
Tresulgan Viaduct 128
Treverrin Tunnel 153
Treviscoe 170
Truro 172

Umberleigh 33
Umborne 58

Wellington 12
Weycroft 62
Whimple 54-55
Whiteball Tunnel 13
Whitford 60
Wilmington 57

Yeoford 26-27